Roadrunners Don't Say Beep-Beep

Simple Wonders of the Desert's Most Famous Bird

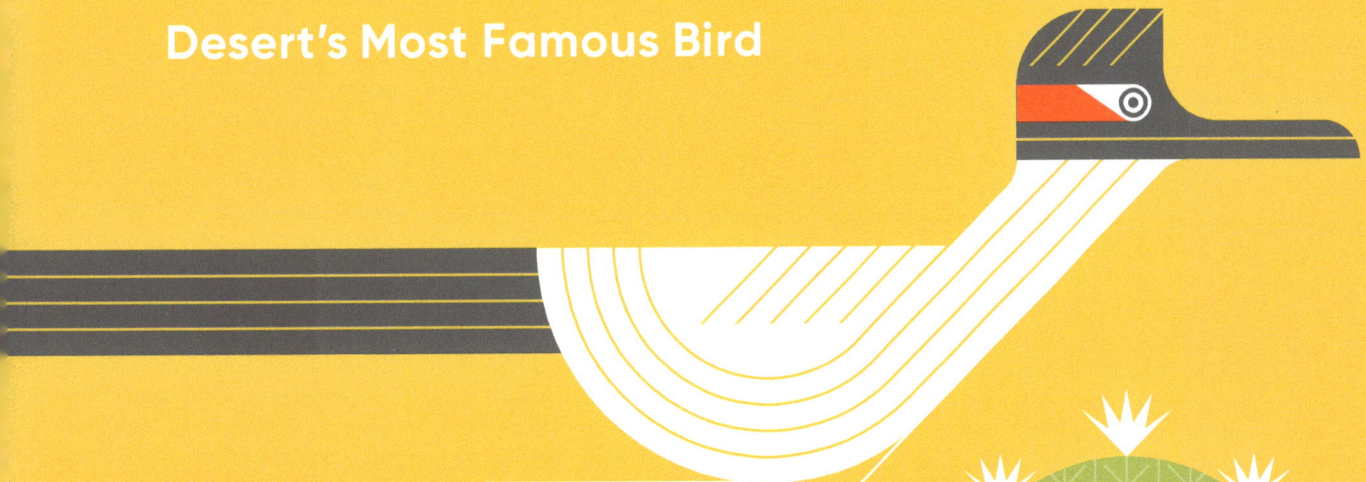

Written and Illustrated
by Bill Chiaravalle

MODERN ROADRUNNER

For all those intrigued and
inspired by the wild and wonders
of the desert's most famous bird.

And to my grandkids Josiah,
Penelope, Vivianne, Jack, Madeleine,
Margeaux, and Samantha.

May you always run after
your dreams.

And finally, to my wife Leila,
thank you for sharing this run
through the desert with me.

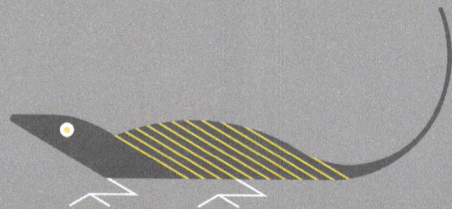

This I know,
that roadrunners
can run fast,
but they fly rather slow.

With tails so long,
and wings too short,

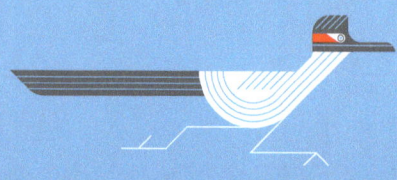

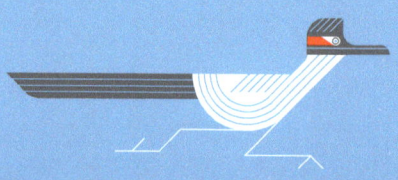

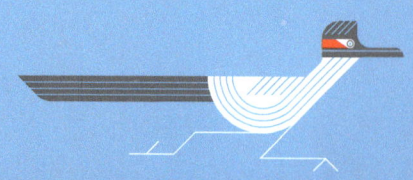

they prefer the ground
for their mode of transport.

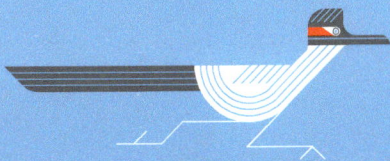

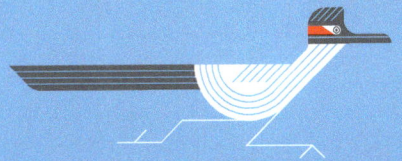

This I have seen
when exploring the desert,

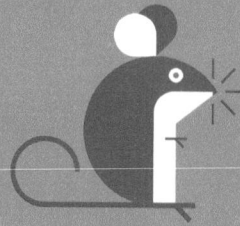

a land of less green
and mostly dry dirt.

But looking closer
at the wonders
of the West,

you'll find these
chaparral birds
with feet like an x.

This I find cool,
what roadrunners eat
to get their fuel.

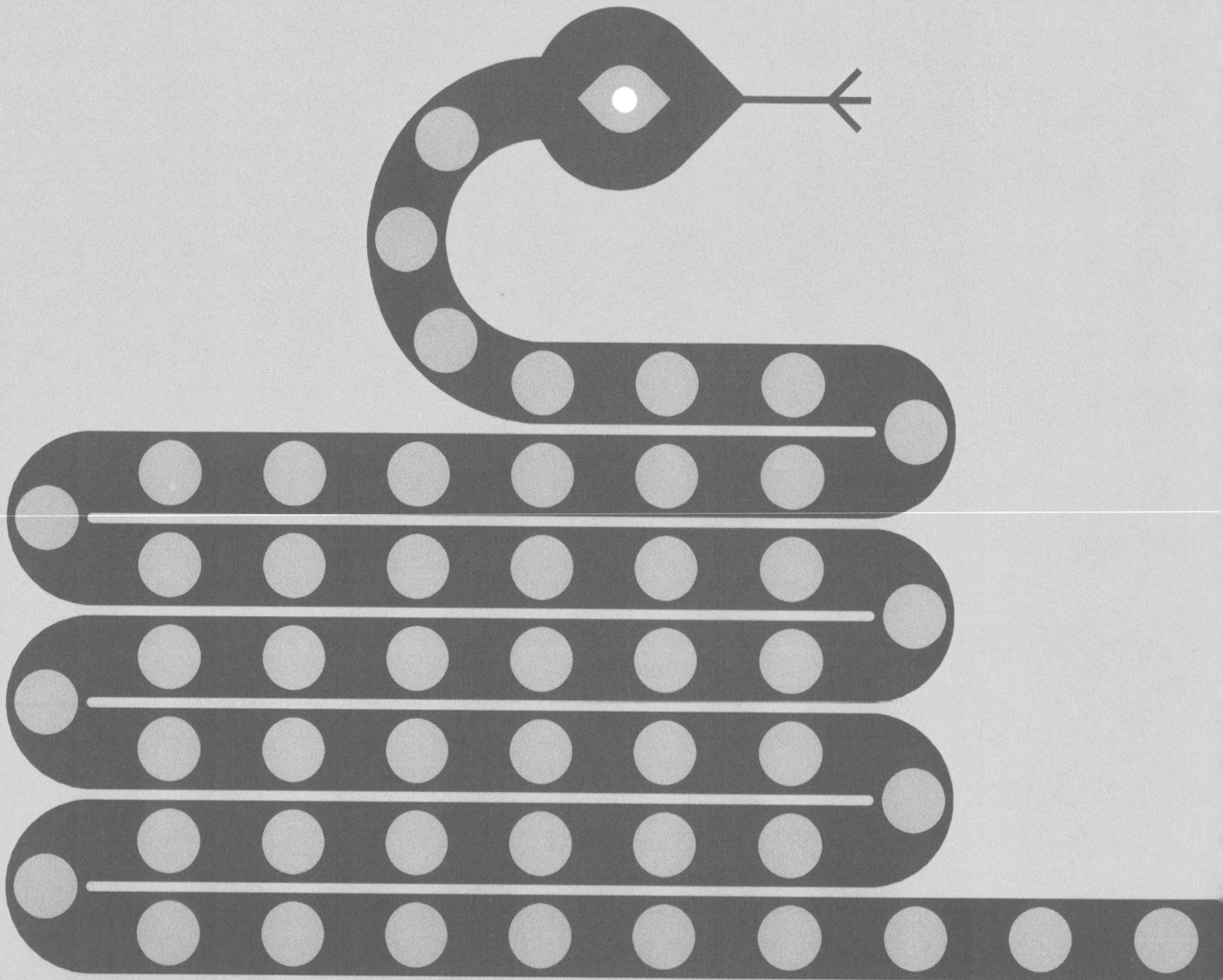

They swallow lizards,
snakes, cactuses, and berries;
what they enjoy
can certainly quite vary.

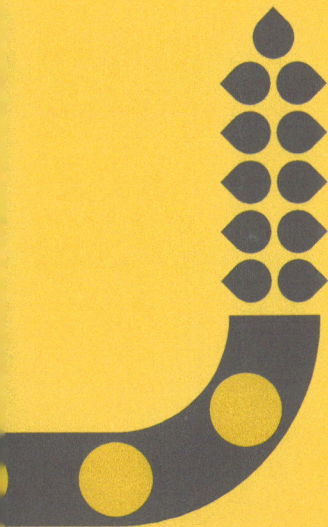

This I do ponder,
why the natives
perceived them as
creatures of wonder.

Hailed for endurance
and extolled for their speed,
these special qualities
are admired in this breed.

In this I delight,
two birds stay together
when others take flight.

Bonded by nature
and mates for life,
they live in one nest
like husband and wife.

And last but not least,
of all that I've learned,
roadrunners are often
more seen than heard.

They may clack their bills
and coo-coo their beaks,
but this is for sure,
they don't say beep-beep!

Roadrunner facts

Roadrunners run **20 mph** and some even faster. Contrary to the cartoon, **coyotes are faster.** They can also catch and will even eat roadrunners.

Roadrunners **can't fly very high** or for long distances. But they can **jump and glide** from one point to another.

Roadrunner couples form **lifelong** bonds that renew each spring with a series of elaborate **courtship** steps and calls.

Roadrunners eat lizards, insects, scorpions, hummingbirds, and even **rattlesnakes.** They also enjoy a variety of fruit, seeds, and plants.

More Roadrunner facts

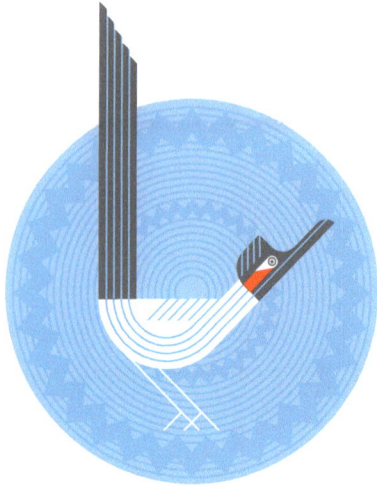

Roadrunners, also known as the "sunrise bird," symbolize the Cahuilla **spirit of enterprise.**

The Cahuilla are a Native American people in the Palm Springs area.

Roadrunners live mostly in the **Southwest** where it is sunny and warm. In the morning, they often sunbathe to warm up after a cool desert night.

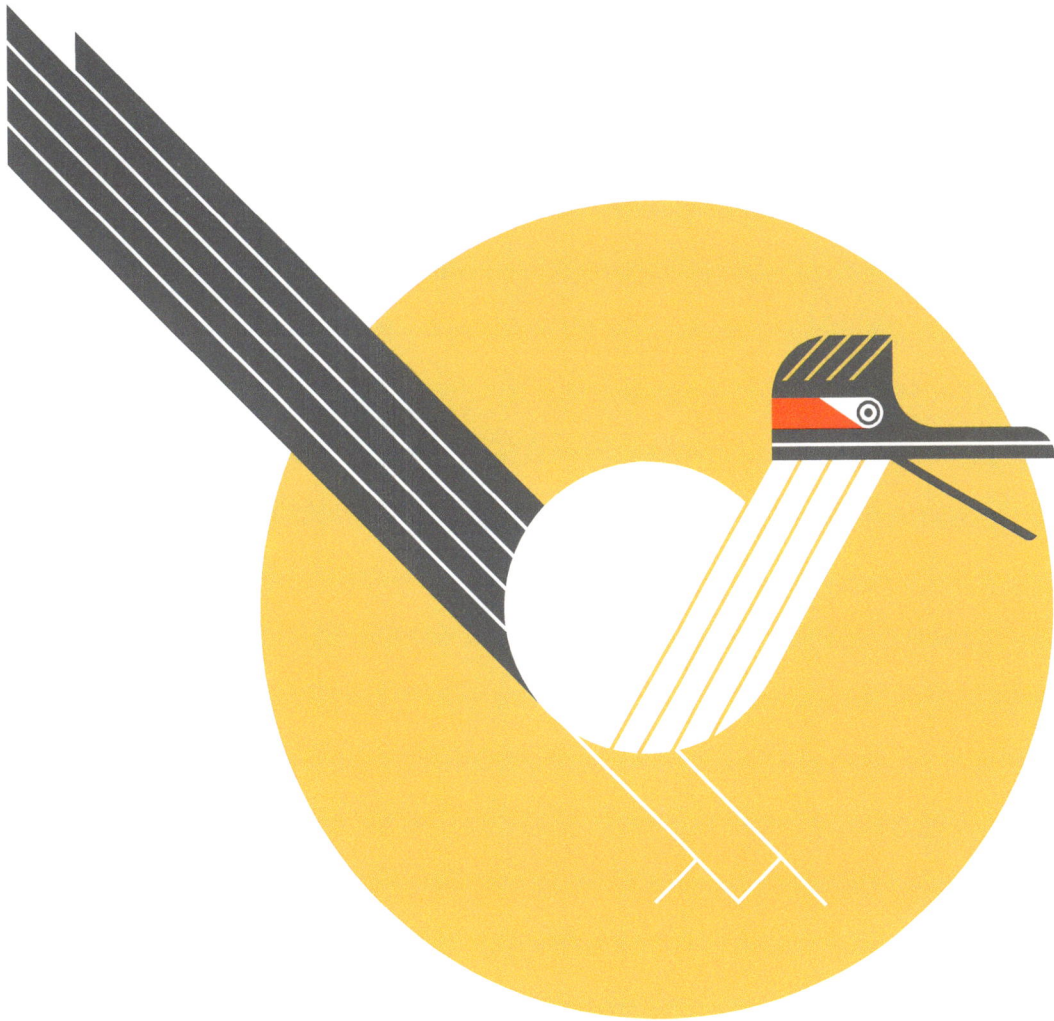

Roadrunners make a distinct clacking and coo-cooo-cooooing sound, but they **never, ever** say "beep-beep."

www.ingramcontent.com/pod-product-compliance
Lightning Source LLC
Chambersburg PA
CBHW042027090426

42811CB00016B/1770